"Shinjo Ito's teachings provide a practice for people with busy lives to follow a path of enlightenment. He taught that the challenges of daily life are themselves opportunities for self-awareness and self-knowledge.

Spiritual practice is the honest and thoughtful scrutiny of one's own attitudes, emotions, and actions. Although this begins with thorough and patient work on oneself, the self is not the goal.

This book of Shinjo's thoughts is useful to all people regardless of religion because it offers a method of compassionate attentiveness to a world in need."

—*Margaret R. Miles, Professor Emerita,*
Graduate Theological Union

"*Though you may have received the body of a human, your mind is like that of a buddha.* These words from the Nirvana Sutra were spoken by the Buddha Shakyamuni to the layman Chunda, who offered the Buddha his last meal. I first came across them many years ago, quoted in one of the earliest texts of Zen. Somehow, they've stuck with me.

Why did the Buddha say that Chunda has the mind of a *buddha*, an awakened being? Because he made an offering. Usually we think that humans give to buddhas, but the Buddha seems to be saying that buddhas give to buddhas.

The way of practice developed by Shinjo Ito derives from the understanding that we may be merely human, but our minds are like that of the Buddha. Therefore, to express our buddha minds as human beings, we make offerings to the other buddhas around us, giving ourselves that all may flourish."

—*Carl Bielefeldt, Professor,*
Stanford University

SHINJO

REFLECTIONS

Published by Somerset Hall Press
416 Commonwealth Avenue, Suite 612
Boston, MA 02215
www.somersethallpress.com

ISBN 978-1-935244-00-4

Editor: Anton Pantzikas
Graphic Design: Julian Peploe + John Lindell

First Edition
Printed in the United States of America on acid-free paper.

Library of Congress Cataloging-in-Publication Data

Ito, Shinjo, 1906-1989.
  Shinjo : reflections / foreword by Her Holiness Keishu Shinso ;
edited and compiled by Anton Pantzikas.
    p. cm.
  ISBN 978-1-935244-00-4
  1. Religious life--Buddhism. I. Pantzikas, Anton. II. Title.
  BQ5395.I86 2009
  294.3´444--dc22
2008052895

contents

Foreword

It is an honor to write a foreword for this book of timeless wisdom.

Shinjo Ito was my father and also my main spiritual teacher. I felt such reverence for him that sometimes I was almost afraid to approach him. And yet at the same time, I adored him.

Shinjo was also a renowned Buddhist sculptor. One day while working in his studio, he encouraged me to make a bust of myself. I was still very young, but I fondly remember him saying, "Look closely at yourself in the mirror. You will begin to find things you didn't see before."

He was teaching me the importance of reflection. It was only later, after I had embarked on my own path, that I realized these words came from his own experience of daily practice.

Our individual lives are made up of what we think, do, and say. When our different lives come together, we form families, society, and the world itself. To develop ourselves spiritually, some of us become ordained or join a monastic order. But it is not necessary for everyone to do so. Our everyday lives can also provide us with enough raw material to make significant spiritual progress. Along the way, it is inevitable that we will sometimes experience unease and doubt. Shinjo realized this and made addressing these challenges the focus of his teaching.

I am grateful that his teachings are now able to reach a wider audience. If the Buddhist insights Shinjo Ito expressed throughout his life and practice can be a source of strength for people to make the most of their lives, then this will give me deep and lasting happiness.

(Keishu) Shinso Ito
Spiritual Head of Shinnyo Buddhism

Master Shinjo Ito (1906-1989) was an artist, photographer, and engineer who is widely regarded as one of the great Buddhist teachers of his time. Born in a rural province of Japan, Shinjo was ordained at Daigoji monastery in the Shingon Buddhist tradition at age 30 and was later recognized as an *acharya*, a teaching master. A husband and father, Shinjo worked tirelessly to make a path of wisdom accessible to all, founding the Shinnyo-en order.

This book is entitled *Shinjo: Reflections*. Shinjo taught that reflection led to awareness, especially of the courage, compassion, and clarity residing in our hearts. He saw happiness as the practical result of kindness and generosity and emphasized these qualities as the foundation of a meaningful life. He also knew that enlightened living was not the sole preserve of Buddhism and saw his mission as simply to give people the tools they needed to transform their lives.

In this book, many of Shinjo's most important thoughts are being made available to a wider English audience for the first time. It is a move of which he would no doubt have approved. One of the hallmarks of his awakening was his willingness to transcend the confines of religion, nationality, and culture. Throughout his life, he learned from many teachers and disciplines: from photography to literature, engineering to human psychology. For Shinjo, anything was useful if it led to direct, experiential contact with the pure, awakened mind. Besides formal teachings, he also made use of poetry, sculpture, and calligraphy to open the wisdom eyes of his students. He sought to help individuals engage compassionately with others, and through the example he set, held forth the universal responsibility we all share for making our planet a happier place to live.

The chapters of this book have been divided into the main areas that Shinjo focused his teachings upon. They are somewhat logically—if loosely—sequenced. Whether Buddhist or not, the reader will find much wisdom here to help negotiate many of life's uncertain situations. The translation has been kept deliberately simple to retain the open spirit of the original Japanese. As a spiritual teacher, Shinjo used simple and direct language to inspire his students to develop their great potential for empathy, kindness, and inner peace. It is my hope that this small book will contribute to the continuation of his noble legacy.

December 2008

Acknowledgments

One thing many people remember about Master Shinjo was the genuine gratitude evident in all his interactions. Only after some years of Buddhist practice did it finally dawn on me that gratitude is one of the simplest ways to happiness.

So in that spirit, let me take this opportunity to thank the people who have contributed to this book. Firstly, I am grateful to Somerset Hall Press, our publisher, who believed in Shinjo's message and did so much to bring the project to fruition. I would also like to thank the members of the Shinnyo-en Foundation in the United States and the Shinnyo-en Head Temple office in Japan who so trustingly and patiently worked with me and lent me their expertise and wisdom. I extend a special thanks to the tireless translators, the volunteers who provided such insightful feedback, and my assistant editor, without whom this book would not have been possible. Most especially, I would like to express my gratitude to Her Holiness Keishu Shinso, the spiritual head of Shinnyo Buddhism, whose guidance and support have been invaluable.

Anton Pantzikas
Editor

VIII

A life of laughter or tears—

the choice is ours.

—*Shinjo*

A Good Life

A Good Life

We all wish for a good life. Some people think all they have to do is believe in a religion. Others think it's about the achievement of material wealth or social status. But I believe that a "good life" is one we can feel good about because of the way we're living it.

3

A Good Life

Such a life is about doing what we know we should do, and the avoidance of doing what we know we should *not* be doing. It is about living a life based on universal truths. This may sound simple to do, but in reality it is not. For example, we know it is not good to be driven by emotion and argue with our partner, children, or parents. Yet we fight with them anyway despite knowing that it's bad.

4

Shakyamuni Buddha said that those who are generous will be blessed with spiritual merit. Those who are kind will not invite grudges. And those who let go of greed will become free from worry. As a Buddhist, I base my life on the truths taught by Buddha Shakyamuni. He used his experiences to awaken himself. Knowledge is not enough. We need to put what we know

5

into practice and learn from experience.

That will naturally lead to living a life we feel

happy with.

If we only view ourselves from a material perspective, it is easy to think that the more we possess or the richer we become, the better our life will be. But no matter how materially blessed we may become, we are still not guaranteed a good life. True fulfillment comes from serving and caring about others, not only ourselves. For me, this ideal is not only admirable; it is how I try to live my life each day.

7

2

Affirmation

What is most important is to go deep into ourselves and discover the loving kindness and compassion of the buddha within–the awakened nature we all possess.

9

Authentic Self

To reflect on everything in daily life is to
nurture your buddha nature.

Authentic Self

When we see that we too have a buddha nature,

we will realize how precious we truly are.

Authentic Self

When we study and practice the teachings of the Buddha we are bodhisattvas—ones who walk a path to buddhahood. So there is no need to ever think negatively about ourselves.

12

People around us serve as mirrors that reflect what we project or perhaps the negative tendencies we, too, have inside of us. When we have thoughts like, "They don't understand," or, "They're giving me a hard time," it is we who are causing ourselves grief, not others. Such moments are opportunities to reflect on our attitude or state of mind.

13

Reflection

We may prefer to deny what we see in the mirror in front of us, but that would be like ignoring the advice of our inner buddha trying to teach us about ourselves.

14

Friends who point out your shortcomings are actually helping you. Appreciate them as if they were showing you the way to a mountain of gold.

15

Reflection

Those who cannot be objective about themselves tend to get caught up in the moment.

16

Those who can look deeply into themselves develop the eyes of wisdom to see not just what is directly in front of them, but also what lies on the road ahead.

17

Reflection

It's better to reflect on your actions than to worry about your luck for the day.

Courage

It takes a lot of courage to let go of our deep-

rooted craving to always want more.

Courage

Attachments and fears give rise to our perceived limitations. Letting them go is to set ourselves free.

Courage

Grass is often trampled on, yet it retains the spirit to grow.

Courage

It is only through the trials of life that we can
achieve true enlightenment.

Courage

We need to know that there are two types of courage. One is ego-driven. The other is not. Egoless courage is to admit our mistakes and shortcomings and to humbly keep going.

23

3

Mindfulness

Words

To teach with kindness benefits both teacher
and student.

Be kind when correcting others, and always do so by first putting yourself in their shoes.

26

Words

Wisdom cannot flow from the mouths of those

who are not mindful of what they say.

Words

Take responsibility for what you say.

28

Words

Do not speak words that are empty of meaning
or full of ego.

Patience

The more we examine ourselves and learn from our mistakes, the clearer our future becomes.

We would all love to be rid of our bad habits, but this requires effort. The first step is for us to understand *and* accept that the causes of such habits lie hidden deep within our minds. Indeed, genuine transformative change occurs only after thorough and patient effort.

31

Patience

As with planting seeds, our efforts will not bear fruit in just one day.

Patience

Once we have resolved to walk the spiritual path, we need to be diligent to see what we should change about ourselves. In particular, we should be aware of the negative traits that obscure our true nature.

Patience

Just as we take time every day to look at
ourselves in the mirror and wash our faces, we
must take time to reflect on ourselves and work
on our character.

Patience

It *is* possible to learn how to recognize and work with the tendencies that hold us back. But it will require effort and patience.

Patience

Living a spiritual life is about more than being selfless. It also means being able to see adversity as opportunity.

36

Time

Time is precious. How many people can say with confidence that they spend their time in a truly meaningful way? We may not be able to achieve something big with our time, but it would be nice if we could say we used it wisely.

37

Time

One who follows the spiritual path should make the most of the "now" that will never come around again.

Time

It is how we use our time *now* that determines the path we take.

4

Poisons

Anger

If all we do is repress our anger, it is like pushing down on a coiled spring. Sooner or later the spring will bounce back.

41

Anger

As ego-driven people, we tend to become angry
and upset over the smallest things.

Anger

If we let our egos run wild, it only makes this already troubled world worse.

Anger

Responding to hatred or anger with more of the same only increases and prolongs our own suffering.

44

Anger

How we react when we're upset is entirely
up to us.

45

Anger

We can react egotistically to what bothers us and become angry and critical. But doing so only creates further suffering.

46

Anger

When we try to understand the viewpoint

of someone who has made us angry, a new

way of looking at the confrontation becomes

possible—as an opportunity to see the situation

for what it really is.

47

Anger

In our search for truth, exasperation can become an obstacle unless we turn it around into an opportunity for a precious spiritual transformation.

Craving

Without realizing it, we are often motivated by greed. The conditioned mind continually craves more, unable to recognize and let go of the attachments that feed this drive.

The way we currently live and build our societies

is centered on the insatiable craving for more.

50

Craving to be well-liked and flattered by others is a form of indulging one's karma. If you want praise, strive to be praised by the wise, not the foolish.

51

Craving

Sometimes when people see a successful person, they either become envious or attribute their success to luck, forgetting the efforts that the person has made to get there.

52

Ignorance

The stronger our ego becomes, the more we view life through a distorted lens. To look at the world clearly, we need the wisdom to see things as they really are.

53

Ignorance

When confronted by something we don't like, we should not be so focused on the form so that we let preconceived notions or external appearances blind us to what is being taught to us at that moment.

Ignorance

Sometimes the eyes we use to see, the ears we use to listen, and the mind we use to think are our biggest obstacles to wisdom.

Ignorance

Many are those who pity others while being
blind to their own misfortune.

Ignorance

Like throwing dust against the wind, when you

act against truth, it will only blow back on you.

Even when the paths that holy men
and women have taken are clear,
people think they themselves cannot
do the same.

—*Shinjo*

5

Making the Most of Life

Making the Most of Life

We cannot feel grounded if we live only for ourselves. Only when we also focus on the well-being of others will our lives be secure and meaningful. Every day I reflect upon how I have been granted life to use selflessly in the service of others, and not only to gratify my own desires.

61

Making the Most of Life

While everyone may agree on the importance of dedicating ourselves to the happiness of others, we may also feel that such an aspiration is very difficult to put into practice. What we can do is first be mindful of those around us by placing ourselves in their position. From there, we act with sincerity and a true desire to help the other person. This means to care about the happiness of those around us, and to make the most of each day by valuing others.

Making the Most of Life

This is how we can make the best use of the Buddha's teachings in everyday life. I firmly believe that through small but continuous efforts, our faith and spiritual practice acquire life and meaning.

63

Making the Most of Life

Modern life provides me with many opportunities to reflect on human nature. For example, our lives have been made more comfortable by developments in science and technology, yet these produce adverse effects that we can all too easily ignore. I have noticed that our pursuit of advanced knowledge seems to interest us more than putting such knowledge to its best use.

64

Sometimes we stop at nothing to pursue an ideal, giving little thought to how our actions affect others. Our life on this planet is a gift to us, so my greatest wish is that we work together in the interests of humanity and the world.

65

6

Heart

Helping

We help ourselves by helping others.

Helping

To be able to help others, we need to put ourselves in their place. We begin by trying to understand them. Then, we try to see things the way they do, even if we think it is impossible. That effort will show in how we interact with them, and that is when our sincere intentions will be felt and received wholeheartedly.

68

Passing judgment on people we think have done wrong is not the way to help them. We must encourage them to seek happiness in the correct way. This will also encourage us to do the same.

Helping

Helping someone spiritually is not the same as helping someone materially. Even if it is only in small ways we should share the joy of the path we've taken. This means to inspire others to lead a spiritual life and find true happiness.

70

Generosity

Without joy, giving is just a physical act. *With*
joy, giving has the power to transform hearts
and minds.

Generosity

Happiness does not come from doting on what we've done for others. Generosity is not about "I".

72

Generosity

It is okay to forget what we have done for

others, but not what they have done for us.

Generosity

To be generous is to act willingly and with joy.

Generosity

True kindness and love are about giving,

not receiving. In giving kindness and love

unconditionally, we receive the same in return.

Love

There are two kinds of love. One is blind—based on craving and the pull of karma. The other involves seeing clearly—based on dharma and truth.

76

77

Heart

7

Awakening

We are on this planet to walk a path of truth.

Enlightenment

The enlightenment of one leads to the enlightenment of countless others.

80

Light

A candle offers itself to give light to people. For a place to become brighter, all it takes is for one candle to light others.

Pride

The voices of buddhas can be found within the cries of human suffering. If we are too proud, we may not be able to hear these noble voices around us.

Listening

Listen to your mother and father. Listen to your husband. Listen to your wife. Listen to the words of your best friends. Listen to everybody. Both to their words of advice and to their suffering. Listen to the cries of the sick, to the wails of anguish and emotion, as well as to the voices of exhilaration. Unless we can listen to our fellow human beings, we will not hear the sublime voice of the universe trying to awaken us.

Gratitude

Gratitude is the first step toward enlightenment.

84

Peace

To attain enlightenment is to gain

unshakable peace.

8

Mind

Mind

Both delusion and enlightenment arise from
the mind.

Creation

Just as art reflects the artist, everything is a creation of the mind.

88

Wisdom

If we can tap into our innate wisdom and
perceive each event that happens around us
as an opportunity to nurture the buds of
our spiritual growth, we will begin to grasp
universal truths.

89

Nirvana

–

Nothing prevents us from reaching the

seemingly far-off shore of nirvana but ourselves.

90

The real hindrances to our spiritual progress are

deep-rooted attachments within us.

Attachment

People so often live their lives ruled by

their attachments.

92

Our minds create the world we live in.

Nirvana means to extinguish the burning
fires of the Three Poisons: greed, anger, and
ignorance. This can be accomplished by
letting go of dissatisfaction.

94

Opportunity

Speculation and constant judging will only limit what you see. Expand your sight by looking at everything in life as an opportunity to develop and transform yourself.

Happiness

Happiness comes from regarding others as buddhas—with humility and love.

96

97

98

How can the state of nirvana (enlightenment) be made accessible to more people? Finding a way is what I have lived for.

—*Shinjo*

9

The Path

The Path

The spiritual path is not mapped out for us to follow. It is a way that only unfolds as we continue to make a conscious effort.

101

The Path

Unlike most Buddhist clergy in Japan, I was not born into a family of priests. I simply aspired to be of help to others and therefore decided to undertake monastic Buddhist training. I resolved to devote my life to developing a path that could lead all beings to true spiritual liberation. I persevered through the deaths of my two sons and also through a difficult period of persecution. But perhaps my greatest challenge lay in trying to develop a way that could lead everyone, without exception, to nirvana (enlightenment). To this end I prayed and meditated countless times.

103

The Path

It is human nature to want to follow an easy path walked by many others. We shy away from anything that seems difficult. However, if there is no path to follow, we have to make one. The harder the circumstances, the more courageous we must become to accomplish what, at the time, may seem impossible. That is when our journey becomes meaningful.

104

10

Practice

Spiritual practice transforms each day and,

eventually, the whole course of our lives.

107

Thinking

We all wish to bring out the best in ourselves.

Thinking too much about it, without acting,

will only leave us feeling lost and confused.

Result

Enlightenment is the result of the daily practice of mindfulness.

Basics

Practice rather than theory is the basis of

pursuing the way to happiness.

Letting go

It is important to let go of our tendency to argue and theorize about everything. Simply walk the path and try your best to be in oneness with the way of the buddhas.

Determination

Walking on the path does not mean we will be completely free from life's problems and difficulties. As we progress and continue striving, some hardships will naturally beset us. But continuing on the path with a firm belief in what we are doing will certainly bring joy in the end.

112

Steady

Regarding our practice, we should neither rush recklessly ahead, nor stand still. We should be neither too loose nor too constricted in our efforts, but simply follow the middle way.

Role Model

Mastering the teachings means to demonstrate in one's deeds what one reads in the scriptures.

Insight meditation (*sesshin*) is not about conceptual thinking or theorizing on a worldly level. It is about embracing the great, fearless mind of the buddhas and bodhisattvas—the great compassion that eases the suffering of all sentient beings—and then putting that into action around us.

115

Keep Going

Enlightenment is a result of our constant effort to keep going.

Sincerity

Sincerity directed toward others accumulates as spiritual merit that we later reap.

11

Karma

Good Karma

Thanks to the good karma we generate from correct meditation, we eventually become able to perceive the universal loving kindness and compassion that is always around us. We can then experience heaven in the here and now, regardless of whether the physical circumstances around us change or remain the same.

Unique Paths

Just as each person's face is distinct, so is their karma and how they pursue the spiritual path.

120

The Smallest Things

The principle of karma is evident even in the smallest things that happen around us each day. However, because they are often minor things, it is easy for us to overlook the law of cause and effect at work.

121

Cause and Effect

The law of cause and effect—or karma—is central to Buddhism and teaches that all phenomena are the result of causes coinciding with conditions.

122

In order for something to exist, it is always subject to a series of interrelationships. This forms the basis of the universe and human life and is the foundation of the Buddha's teachings.

123

Perspective

Everything is the result of one cause or another. In the same way, the present exists because of the past and the future exists because of the present. Make the most of this principle of cause and effect.

124

Perspective

Examine the present and learn from the past to see how the future will unfold. Too often we just look at the present and base our actions solely on that.

The degree to which we have a false sense of reality differs for each of us, depending on how the karmic law of cause and effect is operating in our lives. This is due to both the karma we have created in our present life and the karma from our past. This is why it is important to

continue along the path. There is a Buddhist saying: "If I do not liberate myself now, then when shall I do so?"

Some teach divine punishment, when it's simply
the law of cause and effect.

127

12

Buddhas

True Nature

All sentient beings possess a buddha nature—
their true nature. Therefore all living creatures
have the potential to become a buddha.

Buddha Nature

By working to develop our inherent buddha nature, we can let go of our delusions and attain the state of nirvana, or enlightenment.

Buddha images are not idols to be worshiped. They are physical reminders of our own buddha nature. Through venerating what the image represents, we reconnect our hearts and minds to the love and kindness that buddhas emanate.

131

Cosmic Buddha

Although the Buddha Shakyamuni's physical

body was impermanent, the *dharma body*

(universal truth) at his core is ever-present and

unchanging.

Eternity

Buddhas continue to live on through their teachings as *dharma* bodies. Their spirits become manifest in the *sangha* (spiritual community) where their teachings are passed on.

133

You may have seen people praying to an image as if it had special power. Perhaps they're wishing for the well-being of their family, for material prosperity, or to recover from illness. But this way of practicing faith only leads us to a dead end. Buddha images should serve as inspirations to cultivate the infinite loving kindness latent in the buddha within us.

134

Purpose

The Buddha shared his teachings so that everyone, without exception, could reach the same supreme state of liberation that he had attained through practice and effort.

135

Talking and Doing

It is easy to say we admire the Buddha and want to walk in his footsteps, but talking about it and actually doing it are two very different things.

136

Harmony

The spirit of Buddhism is, more than anything,

about valuing harmony and unity, in which

others are respected and embraced rather than

denounced. This has been the way of Buddhism

since the beginning, and this is true Buddhism.

(From a message delivered on Vatican Radio, June 29, 1967)

137

138

Appendix

My Buddhism

Born into an ordinary family, I never gave any thought in my early years to becoming a priest or religious leader. I was, however, taught an art of spiritual discernment that had been passed down through my family's paternal line. Later, after settling into life as an engineer, I began to use this gift to help those around me solve their problems.

Hoping that Shingon Buddhism could provide a more substantial vehicle for me to help people find real happiness, I entered the priesthood and completed all the training that the monastery provided. However, I then encountered a dilemma. Since Shingon is an esoteric school, it is impossible to provide the same kind of instruction and guidance to others unless they have been formally ordained in the monastic tradition. Therefore, I faced the new challenge of finding the means to teach lay practitioners what I had learned.

With the help of my wife Tomoji, and not knowing where my search would lead, I dedicated myself to developing a method of practice by which lay people could attain the same spiritual level as any priest. I immersed myself in my pursuit, studying the entire Buddhist canon, until one day I realized the potential of the Parinirvana Sutra. My joy and excitement at this discovery is something I will never forget.

In the Sutra there is the phrase, "Encountering this teaching is like a blind sea turtle encountering a floating log with a hole in it, and poking its head through." These words encapsulate how rare it is to encounter the teachings of the Parinirvana Sutra. Indeed, I sensed that something supremely caring and compassionate must have been guiding me toward this discovery. I then committed myself to the path of the buddhas.

The Parinirvana (Nirvana) Sutra is a compilation of
the final teachings that the Buddha Shakyamuni gave
to his disciples before he left his physical body to enter
parinirvana (complete nirvana). Permeating the Sutra
are the concepts that the Buddha is always present in
his teachings and that all sentient beings possess buddha nature. These principles are quite different from
the teachings that Shakyamuni taught earlier in his
life. This is perhaps why in the past there have been
few opportunities to teach a path to enlightenment
based on this sutra.

143

What makes this body of teachings unique are
the events occurring in the parinirvana scene. In it,
we see Shakyamuni surrounded by many monastic
disciples, yet he chooses to give the highest honor to a
lay disciple named Chunda. In the Sutra, he teaches

ways for both lay and monastic practitioners to reach supreme joy, described in the Sutra as the experience of "permanence, bliss, true self, and purity."

Because the Parinirvana Sutra teaches that *anyone* can find liberation, it naturally aims to help as many people as possible to reach it. The Sutra therefore urges its practitioners to become a "Greater Vehicle": someone who helps others to also pursue the way to enlightenment.

For example, in the "Chapter on Bodhisattva Highly Virtuous King," there is the passage:

> *Place others first, then attend to yourself. Act out of the spirit to benefit others, not just yourself.*

The emphasis here is on altruism, on placing the same priority on the happiness of others as one would on one's own.

As human beings, we have the usual tendency to strive for the fulfillment of our own desires first, which is contrary to the teachings of the Buddha. I wrote a verse explaining what it means to be a Greater Vehicle:

Though human, when we dedicate ourselves to others,
We are bodhisattvas.[1]

I would like as many people as possible to experience the state we call "permanence, bliss, true self, and purity." For this to become a reality, I am determined to help my followers awaken to this wish that I hold dear. I hope that we can devote ourselves to the path of the Greater Vehicle, unblinded by self-interest.

---

1 Bodhisattvas are those who have experienced the joy of enlightenment and strive to help others achieve it as well.

Buddhism and Shinnyo-en

Lecture at the University of Oslo, Norway (Excerpted)
June 16, 1967

Buddhism spread across the borders of India and throughout Asia. To explain how Shinnyo-en relates to the development of Buddhism, I would like to mention Nagarjuna, a great sage who lived around the second and third centuries. He left an indelible mark on the history of Buddhism and is believed by many to have formulated the basic principles that led to the establishment of "esoteric" Buddhism.

Nagarjuna examined deeply the spirit of Shakyamuni Buddha, and there he discovered mystical truth. Nagarjuna systematized his discovery into a theory and a way of training oneself. He referred to the mystical truth and psycho-spiritual element of Shakyamuni Buddha's path as esotericism, and to the philosophical element as exotericism.

The esoteric tradition was later transmitted to China, and the great Japanese master, Kukai, brought

146

it to Japan in the year 806. Buddhism had first been introduced into Japan around the sixth century. However, what was transmitted at that time was only an abridged form. It took almost another 300 years for esoteric Buddhism, the spiritual substance of buddhahood, to reach Japan.

The esoteric Buddhism introduced to Japan by Kukai was established as the Shingon ("true-word" or "mantra") school of Buddhism. It has continued to exist as such until the present day. I myself trained in the *Shingon* school and in it could master the Buddha's spiritual, or mystical, teachings. In Buddhist terms, this attainment is described as undergoing "dharma transmission initiation," or becoming a successor of the dharma lineage.

Eventually I studied all the scriptures attributed to Shakyamuni Buddha and became aware of the potential of the Nirvana Sutra. This Sutra was a compilation of the Buddha's final teachings, intended as a "last will and testament," advising how his disciples should carry on after he left this world.

Shakyamuni Buddha had revealed his teachings gradually and adapted them according to the needs of the listener or the occasion. At the final moment of his *parinirvana*—his final passing into complete nirvana—the essence of his spiritual being, or what we can call the core of Buddhism, was revealed for the first time.

148　　Though Shinnyo-en has a high regard for all the teachings expounded over time by Buddhism's various enlightened practitioners, we look to the Nirvana Sutra for the basic philosophical grounding on which we have developed our practice.

In Buddhism there is the concept we call the "unity of the Three Jewels." The term *Three Jewels* refers to

"Buddha-Dharma-Sangha." Buddha is the "buddha spirit"[1]; *Dharma* is the Buddhist scriptures; and *Sangha* is the spiritual community of practitioners who explain the scriptures and embody them in their daily lives. None of these three should be emphasized separately as being superior to the other two.

The "buddha spirit" refers to the sublime. We can only understand it through what is revealed in the scriptures. However, the scriptures cannot be understood without the presence of a *sangha*, a spiritual community, or a person of wisdom to guide us on the path. Therefore, the presence of the Buddha—or "buddha nature"—does not exist apart from the scriptures and the spiritual community. They are

---

1   Buddhahood; the essential, ineffable substance of a buddha that cannot be expressed in mere words.

inextricably linked, as Shakyamuni Buddha himself stated two and half millennia ago.

In Buddhism, we say "all beings inherently possess buddha nature." Therefore, each living thing has the same nature as the Buddha and the potential to become a buddha. This is also a major theme of the Nirvana Sutra. The word *buddha* does not merely signify Shakyamuni Buddha. It refers to one having Shakyamuni Buddha's nature or spirit, or that of a similarly awakened being.

Therefore in Buddhism there is no absolute being or absolute experience that we regard as separate from ourselves. Buddhism regards everything, including each of us, as living an interrelated existence. Hence Shakyamuni Buddha is not an absolute being, nor an intermediary for an absolute being. In the Nirvana Sutra—which we view as the teaching that expresses the Buddha's final wishes and his hopes for those who follow after him—the Buddha says, "After my passing, rely on the teachings that I have expounded—the Dharma—and then train yourselves accordingly."

To "rely" on the teachings does not mean we should regard them as absolute, as things simply to be revered. Shakyamuni Buddha wanted each of his disciples to polish and elevate him or herself spiritually through the teachings he left to them. However, in this lies a danger that as we try to grasp the buddha spirit, we will distort that true spirit by viewing the teachings through our own filter of self-serving ideas. In order to prevent this, a good teacher and guided meditation become necessary to help us see our subjective self from an objective point of view.

Many people believe in the idea that everything is interrelated. The Nirvana Sutra contains the concept

151

of *shoju* (Skt. *parigraha*), which encourages us to "receive, take in, embrace, and acknowledge others," with the hope of helping them. A phrase in the Sutra describes this principle: "All rivers eventually flow into the ocean and become one with it." Therefore, in Shinnyo-en we reject ideas that cause division, such as calling other religious views "heresy." This, I believe, is in line with the teachings of Shakyamuni Buddha. It is how Buddhism should be. It also relates to another view I share: "Truth is revealed in all faiths."

152   For more than 10 years, I have been making Buddhist images. I wanted to give people an opportunity to grasp the buddha spirit through some tangible physical form. Through the image I have presented to you, I hope to express my devotion to the Buddha, and further, to all that is sacred—something we share with all people of faith.

At Shinnyo-en, it is our sincere wish to work hand-in-hand with others, in whatever small way we can, towards peace in the world. This, I believe, reflects the true buddha spirit.

Bodhisattva

(Skt. lit. "enlightenment being")

One who forgoes entry into complete nirvana in order to guide others to spiritual awakening. Earthly bodhisattvas stand out from other people because of their compassion and dedication to helping others.

Buddha

(Skt. lit. "awakened one")

The term buddha refers to 1) a human being who, through diligent practice in accordance with Buddhism's universal laws of truth, has reached a spiritual awakening that allows him or her to permanently transcend the endless ingrained patterns that bind a person to the realms of suffering; 2) transcendental figures (also called "avatars" or "emanations") that represent aspects of buddhahood (buddha nature); 3) the historical person named Shakyamuni who became fully enlightened.

154

Buddhism

A path of spiritual transformation that is grounded in the Buddhist practitioner's own daily practice and experience. Those who "take refuge" (seek liberating truth) in the Buddha's teachings do so with the conscious wish to awaken to their true nature, the essence of which is held by Buddhists to be unfettered wisdom and compassion. Buddhists practice meditation to gain insight, but what is felt to bring true peace and contentment is its application in daily life.

Buddhists believe this is what it means to be a "follower" of the Buddhist path, and to have a direct, personal experience of truth.

Buddhism was founded 2,500 years ago in India by a man named Siddhartha Gautama. Although he had been raised in luxurious surroundings as a prince, Siddhartha came to recognize the harsh and inescapable realities of life. Wanting to cut through the conditioning that prevented him from seeing the universe as it really is, and to free himself from unnecessary suffering, he left his palace to become a wandering ascetic and mendicant. After years of seeking spiritual truth and engaging in punishing ascetic practices, he found a middle road that allowed him to go into deep meditation and awaken fully to his true nature. This made him a buddha, i.e., one who is completely awakened or enlightened.

The word "buddha" is therefore not used to refer to an omniscient creator/god. It can describe an individual who has a deep awareness of the truths that make the universe what it is, as well as that person's unconditioned essence, free and untainted by karma. The universal principles that such a person embodies and teaches—known to Buddhists as "dharma"—are a guide for others on the road to transcending human suffering, both mundane and spiritual.

Fundamental to Buddhism is its reverence for all life. It teaches that striving with an altruistic mindset is essential for true awakening to occur.

Daigoji

The head monastery of the Daigo branch of the Shingon school of esoteric Buddhism. The monastery was founded in 874 in Kyoto by the priest Shobo. In 1976, Shinjo presided over celebrations for the monastery's 1,100th year.

Dharma
This Sanskrit term can have many meanings: cosmic law; teachings that express universal truths; norms or ethical behavior; manifestation of reality or any phenomenon; or, very generally, concepts that reflect what is in the human mind.

Esoteric Buddhism
(also, the Vajrayana or "Diamond Vehicle," and the "secret" or "mystical" teachings)

A system of training that focuses on the acquisition of "unrevealed" wisdom that cannot be understood simply through study. The term "esoteric" (or secret/mystical) is used because training also involves rituals and practices that are only accessed through initiations given by a master who judges when a disciple is ready to receive them. Another reason for the term is that people are believed to be already fully enlightened at the intrinsic level of their buddha nature, but because of their inability to access their innate wisdom, their spiritual knowledge remains hidden.

156   Shinjo described the esoteric teachings as "a fundamental part of Buddhism: its spiritual and psychological core."

Although esoteric Buddhism originated in India and spread to many parts of Asia, it survives as a distinct tradition only in Tibetan Buddhism and in Japan's Shingon, Tendai, and Shinnyo schools.

Exoteric Buddhism
The aspect of Buddhist teachings based upon the logic and theories outlined in the oral and written traditions. These

teachings are defined as exoteric because they are explicitly revealed and can therefore be understood intellectually.

Karma
(Skt. lit. "deed")
Karma refers to the universal principle of "cause and effect," as well as to the conditions that trigger a latent cause to manifest itself as a certain effect. Buddhism says that all phenomena are the results of causes and circumstances that allow the causes to be manifested. Without exception, all beings are inextricably linked to such interrelationships. Karma (cause and effect) is fundamental to understanding the Buddha's teachings regarding the sources of suffering and ultimate liberation from patterns of behavior and thought that continue to create karma.

Nirvana
(Skt. lit. "extinction")
The ultimate objective of all Buddhist pursuits, nirvana refers to a state of joy and wisdom by which a person has found the means to end needless suffering and its causes. Liberated from the determining effect of karma, one enters a different mode of existence which can be described in many ways, such as the bliss of identifying with the absolute, or as total freedom from attachment to illusions and afflictive passions. Such complete liberation, which defies verbal description, is also called *parinirvana*.

157

Parinirvana
(Skt. "complete" or "perfect" nirvana)
Parinirvana can be described as a final release or the infinite nirvana that awaits all buddhas after their physical death. In

a broader sense, the term is associated with one of the most important Mahayana discourses: The Great Parinirvana (Mahaparinirvana) Sutra, which was compiled sometime around the third century. The Sutra's name is often abbreviated simply to "Nirvana Sutra."

Parinirvana image
(also, "nirvana image")
Parinirvana images depict the Buddha in two ways, 1) just before his death, when he was expounding his final teachings and lying on his right side with his head reclining on his right arm; 2) just after leaving his physical body, in which his eyes are closed and he is lying flat on his side. In paintings of this scene, he is often shown surrounded by grieving disciples.

"Permanence, Bliss, True Self, and Purity"
This phrase represents the "four merits" or qualities of nirvana that are highlighted in the Parinirvana Sutra. From this perspective, enlightenment is described as the realization within one's heart of an ever joyful and pure self that is able to disengage from ego. The phrase also describes the attainment of absolute freedom, unswayed by emotions good or bad, and clarity of understanding beyond false views and superficial distinctions.

Shakyamuni
The historical Buddha and founder of Buddhism, Shakyamuni (563–483 BCE) was born Siddhartha Gautama in the town of Kapilavastu in what is now Nepal. He lived the first 29 years of his life as a pampered, wealthy prince before a series of seemingly random and disturbing encounters started him thinking about

the eternal cycle of death and suffering. He renounced his earlier, worldly life and set forth upon a spiritual quest that achieved fruition when he realized complete enlightenment at the age of 35.

Shakyamuni then spent the rest of his life teaching what he had realized, guiding his followers on the spiritual path to self-realization and the discovery of one's buddha nature.

Shinnyo
(Skt. Tathata)
A synonym for "buddha nature" and a term for the ultimate reality at the core of all phenomena, material as well as conceptual. Often translated as "thusness," "suchness," or "as-it-is-ness," shinnyo is a concept that can only be directly experienced and not logically understood. It is the fundamental, primordial nature out of which all phenomena arise.

Shinnyo-en
A Buddhist denomination originally established in Japan in 1936 by Shinjo and Tomoji Ito. Its name literally means "place of *shinnyo*," but refers to a spiritual community open to everyone to discover their shinnyo (see separate entry above), or true nature. Through its various temples, training centers, and private homes, it is a fellowship of instruction and pursuit, in which all people regardless of age, gender, nationality, or religious background can gather to cultivate their innate buddha nature, the kernel of enlightenment existing in all beings.

For a comprehensive overview of Shinjo Ito's life and art please visit www.shinjoito.com.

The author's proceeds from the sale of this book will go to support the work of the Shinnyo-en Foundation. The Foundation aims to build more caring communities by providing grants and support to various organizations worldwide. For more information on their work, please visit www.sef.org.